HOW DOES IT FEEL
TO BE A TREE?

WRITTEN BY **FLO MORSE**

ILLUSTRATED BY **CLYDE WATSON**

PARENTS' MAGAZINE PRESS

NEW YORK

Text copyright © 1976 by Flo Morse
Illustrations copyright © 1976 by Clyde Watson
All rights reserved
Printed in the United States of America

Library of Congress Cataloging in Publication Data
Morse, Flo.
   How does it feel to be a tree?
   SUMMARY: Exploration in verse of what
it must be like to be a tree
   [1. Trees-Poetry] I. Watson, Clyde. II. Title.
PZ8.3.M838Ho   811′.5′4   75-19177
ISBN 0-8193-0829-3   ISBN 0-8193-0830-7 lib. bdg.

For Megan

How does it feel
to be a tree...

High in the sky

and low down with me?

How does it feel
to hold a swing
and hear birds sing
in your branches?

Is it nice
when robins
build nests in you?
And squirrels, too?

What is it like
to bend and sway
but not be able
to run away?

Do you get stiff
standing straight
while you wait
for the wind to blow?

How does it feel
to wear leaves?
Like sleeves?

Are you cold in the fall

with no leaves
at all?

Is snow like a sweater,
only wetter?

Is ice like my slicker,
only thicker?

I wonder if bark
feels like skin.
Does a tree house hurt
moving in?

Does rain tickle?
Do bugs itch?
Which?

Does it feel good
to be wood?
Are you happy
when you're sap-py?

Do you like it
when squirrels scurry
over you
in such a hurry?

Are they wood wreckers,
like woodpeckers?

Is it fun
when you're stirred
by a breeze?

Can you feel one coming—
like a sneeze?

Which wind
do trees
like best?
North, south,
east or west?

How does it feel
to give someone shade?

Is that the real reason
you were made?

When you save a cat
from a dog,
are you glad?

When you catch a kite
from a kid,
are you sad?

Is it frightening
in thunder and lightning
when no one's
supposed to
get close to you?

Are you scared
of bats and owls
and everything
that prowls
round you in the night?

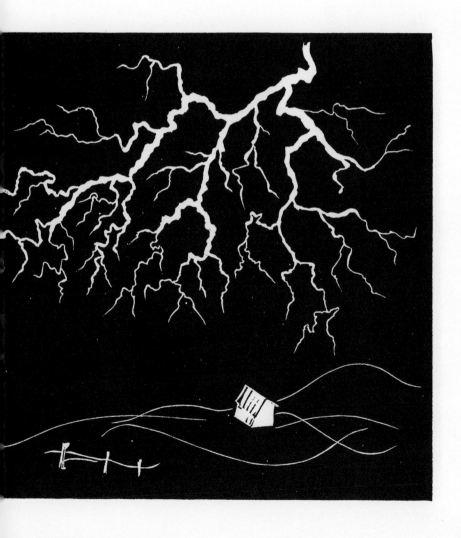

Won't it be hard
when you're old
and dead
to keep standing up
instead of lying down?

When you're tired
and fall,
will they haul you away?

Will you mind
being just a stump?

I'll jump over you—
or will I be too old
then, too?

Are you listening, tree?

Are your leaves
whispering to me?

Will you be lonesome
when I go?

Tell me, so I'll know
how it feels to be a tree.

Long walks through the woods and fields of Bedford Village, New York, led *Flo Morse* "to my own wondering about how it feels to be a rooted tree. The child in all of us speculates about these tongue-tied monuments of nature." The mother of two grown sons, Mrs. Morse has written one work of non-fiction for teenagers about early American communes. This is her first picture book.

Clyde Watson "grew up in Putney, Vermont, with trees as my friends." Her half-dozen previous picture books, including the much-acclaimed *Father Fox's Pennyrhymes,* billed Clyde as author, her sister Wendy as illustrator. This first appearance on the Parents' Magazine Press list also marks Clyde's distinguished debut as a picture-book illustrator. The artist now lives in New Hampshire.